Best of Toto

Contents

Cover art by Levin Pfeufer

Cherry Lane Music Company
Director of Publications/Project Editor: Mark Phillips
Project Coordinator: Rebecca Skidmore

ISBN 978-1-60378-155-8

Visit our website at www.cherrylaneprint.com

99

Words and Music by
David Paich

Moderate Jazz-Rock beat

Nine - ty - nine, I've been wait - ing ___ so long. ___
Nine - ty - nine, I keep break - ing ___ your heart. ___

oh, we were so sure. Oh,__ nine - ty -

nine,   I love __ you.

Repeat and fade

Africa

Words and Music by
David Paich and Jeff Porcaro

7

ech - o - in' to-night.____ She hears on - ly whis - pers of some

qui - et con - ver - sa - tion.

She's com - ing in, twelve thir - ty flight.____
The wild dogs cry out in the night,____ as

Moon - lit wings____ re - flect the stars____ that guide me toward sal - y
they grow rest - less, long - ing for____ some sol - i - tar - y

He turned to me as if to say,
I seem to cure what's deep inside,

"Hurry, boy, it's waiting there for you."
frightened of this thing that I've become.

It's gonna take a lot
to drag me away from you.

There's noth-ing that a hun-dred men __ or more __ could ev - er do. __

I bless the rains __ down in Af -

ri - ca. __ Gon - na take some time __

to do __ the things we nev - er had. __

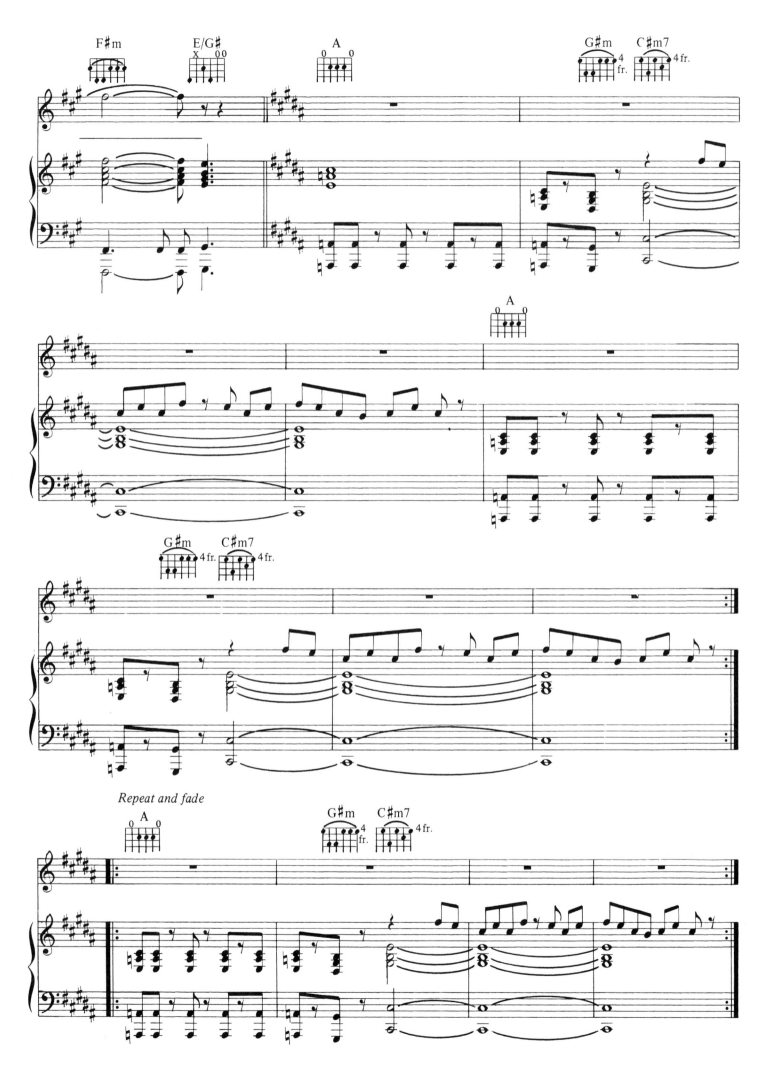

Georgy Porgy

Words and Music by
David Paich

an ad - dict for your love. ___
il - lu - sion. Can't you see? ___

I'm not the on - ly one that holds ___ you. I nev-er, ev - er should have told ___

you you're my on - ly girl. ___

I'm not the on - ly one that holds ___ you. I nev-er, ev - er should have told ___

14

Hold the Line

Words and Music by
David Paich

It's not in the way you say you care.
It's not in the way you say you're mine.

It's not in the way you've been treat - in' my friends.
It's not in the way that you came back to me.

It's not in the way that you stay till the end.
It's not in the way that your love set me free.

It's not in the way you look or the things that you say that you do.
It's not in the way you look or the things that you say that you do.

Hold the

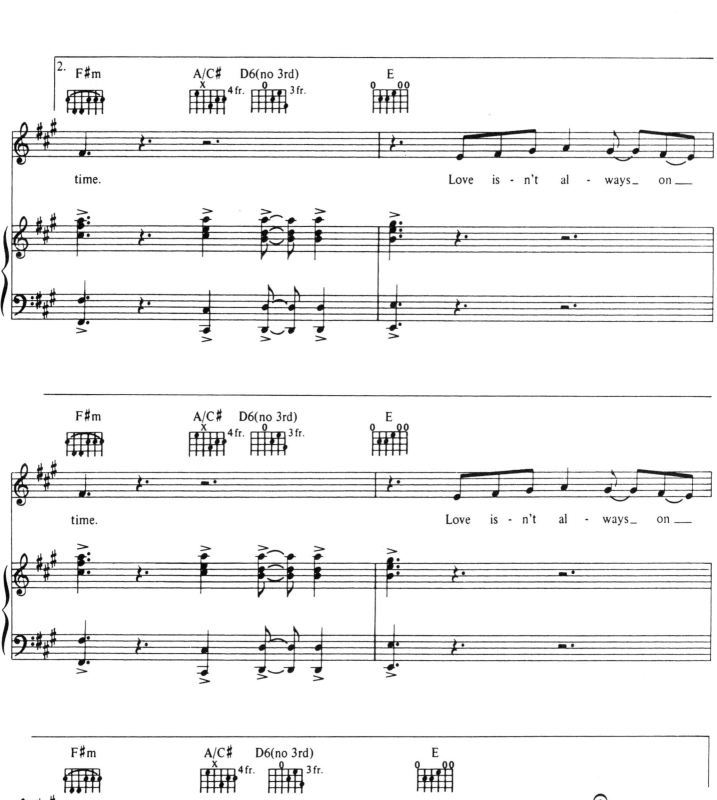

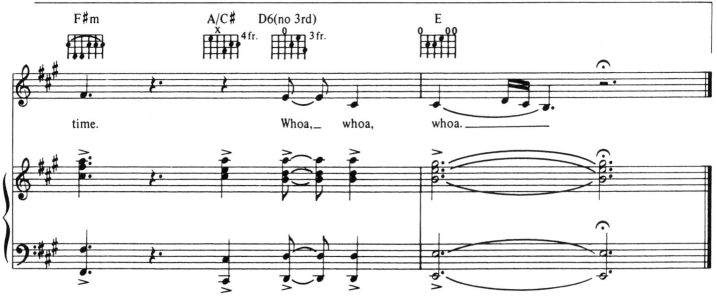

Holyanna

Words and Music by
David Paich and Jeffrey Porcaro

Ho - ly - a - ee - an - na,— girl, you're a blue - eyed mys - ter - y.

To Coda ⊕

1.

You

24

25

I Won't Hold You Back

Words and Music by
Steve Lukather

now.   The love we _ had

just can't _ be found. _   You

know I _ can't hold you _ back now.

Now that I'm _ a - lone,

28

I'll Be over You

Words and Music by
Steve Lukather and Randy Goodrum

guar - an - tees, ____ There are ____ no al - i - bis. ____
time gone ____ by, ____ prom - is - es we ____ once made.

That's how ____ our love must ____ be, ____ don't ask ____ why, ____
What are ____ the rea - sons ____ why ____ noth - in' stays ____ the

same?
There were ____ the nights
It takes ____ some time,

God knows how long. I know that I can for-get you as soon as my
hold-in' you close. Some-day I'll try to for-get them as soon as my

Chorus

heart stops break-in', an-ti-ci-

pa-tin', as soon as for-ev-er is through, I'll be ov-er you.

1.

3. Re-mem-ber-in'

2.

I'll Supply the Love

Words and Music by
David Paich

Must be the chang - in' of the sea - sons.
Could be my first and last oc - ca - sion.

You sup - ply the night, ba - by.

I'll sup - ply the love. You sup - ply the night,

ba - by. I'll sup - ply the love.

I'll sup - ply the love. _____

Make Believe

Words and Music by
David Paich

We went our sep - 'rate ways. _ No
You took it all a - way. _ I
No more pre - tend - in'. _____

mat - ter which way the wind ___ blows now, hang on to it an - y - how.
did - n't come here to change ___ your mind, lead you on, or waste ___ your time.

1.

Don't ev - er say it could nev - er be the same. _____

41

Why don't we make be - lieve? ___

Repeat and fade

Pamela

Words and Music by
David Paich and Joseph Williams

Rosanna

Words and Music by
David Paich

Eb(addF)

Dm9

I did-n't know you were look-in' for more___ than I could ev-er be.
I nev-er thought that ___ los-in'___ you___ could ev-er hurt so bad.

Gm

Not quite a year ___ since you

F/A   Bb   Eb/Bb   Bb   F

went a-way,___   Ro-san na,_____ yeah.___

Gm

Now she's gone, and I

Stop Loving You

Words and Music by
Steve Lukather and David Paich

Time pas - ses quick - ly_ and chan - ces_ are _ few. I won't

stop till_ I'm through lov - ing you,_ girl._

you,_ girl._

Play 3 times
No Chord

Stranger in Town

Words and Music by
David Paich and Jeffrey Porcaro

My heart skipped a beat.
What can they do?

better watch out, there's a stranger in town.

better watch out, there's a stranger in town.

better watch out when he comes a - round.

young girl says it's Je - sus___ and he won't be back___ a - gain___

___ to - night.___ I won - der who's

right.___ You bet - ter watch out,___ there's a

stran - ger in___ town. You bet - ter watch out,___ there's a
(both times) (You bet - ter watch out.)

stran-ger in town. You bet-ter watch out when he comes a -
(2nd time only) (You bet-ter watch out.)

round. You

Don't make a sound.

Repeat and fade
N.C.

Oh.

great songs series

This legendary series has delighted players and performers for generations.

Great Songs of the Fifties

Features rock, pop, country, Broadway and movie tunes, including: All Shook Up • At the Hop • Blue Suede Shoes • Dream Lover • Fly Me to the Moon • Kansas City • Love Me Tender • Misty • Peggy Sue • Rock Around the Clock • Sea of Love • Sixteen Tons • Take the "A" Train • Wonderful! Wonderful! • and more. Includes an introduction by award-winning journalist Bruce Pollock.
02500323 P/V/G..$16.95

Great Songs of the Sixties, Vol. 1 – Revised

The updated version of this classic book includes 80 faves from the 1960s: Angel of the Morning • Bridge over Troubled Water • Cabaret • Different Drum • Do You Believe in Magic • Eve of Destruction • Monday, Monday • Spinning Wheel • Walk on By • and more.
02509902 P/V/G..$19.95

Great Songs of the Sixties, Vol. 2 – Revised

61 more '60s hits: California Dreamin' • Crying • For Once in My Life • Honey • Little Green Apples • MacArthur Park • Me and Bobby McGee • Nowhere Man • Piece of My Heart • Sugar, Sugar • You Made Me So Very Happy • and more.
02509904 P/V/G..$19.95

Great Songs of the Seventies, Vol. 1 – Revised

This super collection of 70 big hits from the '70s includes: After the Love Has Gone • Afternoon Delight • Annie's Song • Band on the Run • Cold as Ice • FM • Imagine • It's Too Late • Layla • Let It Be • Maggie May • Piano Man • Shelter from the Storm • Superstar • Sweet Baby James • Time in a Bottle • The Way We Were • and more.
02509917 P/V/G..$19.95

Great Songs of the Seventies, Vol. 2

Features 58 outstanding '70s songs in rock, pop, country, Broadway and movie genres: American Woman • The Loco-Motion • My Eyes Adored You • New Kid in Town • Night Fever • Summer Breeze • Tonight's the Night • We Are the Champions • Y.M.C.A. • more. Includes articles by Cherry Lane Music Company founder Milt Okun, and award-winning music journalist Bruce Pollock.
02500322 P/V/G..$19.95

Great Songs of the Eighties – Revised

This edition features 50 songs in rock, pop & country styles, plus hits from Broadway and the movies! Songs: Almost Paradise • Angel of the Morning • Do You Really Want to Hurt Me • Endless Love • Flashdance...What a Feeling • Guilty • Hungry Eyes • (Just Like) Starting Over • Let Love Rule • Missing You • Patience • Through the Years • Time After Time • Total Eclipse of the Heart • and more.
02502125 P/V/G..$18.95

Great Songs of the Nineties

Includes: Achy Breaky Heart • Beautiful in My Eyes • Believe • Black Hole Sun • Black Velvet • Blaze of Glory • Building a Mystery • Crash into Me • Fields of Gold • From a Distance • Glycerine • Here and Now • Hold My Hand • I'll Make Love to You • Ironic • Linger • My Heart Will Go On • Waterfalls • Wonderwall • and more.
02500040 P/V/G..$16.95

Great Songs of Broadway

This fabulous collection of 60 standards includes: Getting to Know You • Hello, Dolly! • The Impossible Dream • Let Me Entertain You • My Favorite Things • My Husband Makes Movies • Oh, What a Beautiful Mornin' • On My Own • People • Tomorrow • Try to Remember • Unusual Way • What I Did for Love • and dozens more, plus an introductory article.
02500615 P/V/G..$19.95

Great Songs of Classic Rock

Nearly 50 of the greatest songs of the rock era, including: Against the Wind • Cold As Ice • Don't Stop Believin' • Feels like the First Time • I Can See for Miles • Maybe I'm Amazed • Minute by Minute • Money • Nights in White Satin • Only the Lonely • Open Arms • Rikki Don't Lose That Number • Rosanna • We Are the Champions • and more.
02500801 P/V/G..$19.95

Great Songs of the Country Era

This volume features 58 country gems, including: Abilene • Afternoon Delight • Amazed • Annie's Song • Blue • Crazy • Elvira • Fly Away • For the Good Times • Friends in Low Places • The Gambler • Hey, Good Lookin' • I Hope You Dance • Thank God I'm a Country Boy • This Kiss • Your Cheatin' Heart • and more.
02500503 P/V/G..$19.95

Great Songs of Folk Music

Nearly 50 of the most popular folk songs of our time, including: Blowin' in the Wind • The House of the Rising Sun • Puff the Magic Dragon • This Land Is Your Land • Time in a Bottle • The Times They Are A-Changin' • The Unicorn • Where Have All the Flowers Gone? • and more.
02500997 P/V/G..$19.95

Great Songs from The Great American Songbook

52 American classics, including: Ain't That a Kick in the Head • As Time Goes By • Come Fly with Me • Georgia on My Mind • I Get a Kick Out of You • I've Got You Under My Skin • The Lady Is a Tramp • Love and Marriage • Mack the Knife • Misty • Over the Rainbow • People • Take the "A" Train • Thanks for the Memory • and more.
02500760 P/V/G..$16.95

Great Songs of the Movies

Nearly 60 of the best songs popularized in the movies, including: Accidentally in Love • Alfie • Almost Paradise • The Rainbow Connection • Somewhere in My Memory • Take My Breath Away (Love Theme) • Three Coins in the Fountain • (I've Had) the Time of My Life • Up Where We Belong • The Way We Were • and more.
02500967 P/V/G..$19.95

Great Songs of the Pop Era

Over 50 hits from the pop era, including: Every Breath You Take • I'm Every Woman • Just the Two of Us • Leaving on a Jet Plane • My Cherie Amour • Raindrops Keep Fallin' on My Head • Time After Time • (I've Had) the Time of My Life • What a Wonderful World • and more.
02500043 Easy Piano..$16.95

Great Songs of the Pop/Rock Era

65 fabulous pop/rock favorites in piano/vocal/guitar format. Includes: Africa • Annie's Song • If • Imagine • Jack and Diane • Lady in Red • Oh, Pretty Woman • Respect • Rock Around the Clock • (Sittin' On) The Dock of the Bay • Tears in Heaven • Time in a Bottle • Yesterday • and more.
02500552 P/V/G..$19.95

Great Songs of the 2000s

Over 50 of the decade's biggest hits so far, including: Accidentally in Love • Breathe (2 AM) • Daughters • Hanging by a Moment • The Middle • The Remedy (I Won't Worry) • Smooth • A Thousand Miles • and more.
02500922 P/V/G..$19.99

Great Songs for Weddings

A beautiful collection of 59 pop standards perfect for wedding ceremonies and receptions, including: Always and Forever • Amazed • Beautiful in My Eyes • Can You Feel the Love Tonight • Endless Love • Love of a Lifetime • Open Arms • Unforgettable • When I Fall in Love • The Wind Beneath My Wings • and more.
02501006 P/V/G..$19.95

Prices, contents, and availability subject to change without notice.

cherry lane
music company

www.cherrylane.com

EXCLUSIVELY DISTRIBUTED BY
HAL•LEONARD CORPORATION
7777 W. BLUEMOUND RD. P.O. BOX 13819 MILWAUKEE, WI 53213

0409

More Great Piano/Vocal Books

FROM CHERRY LANE

For a complete listing of Cherry Lane titles available, including contents listings, please visit our web site at

www.cherrylane.com

See your local music dealer or contact:

EXCLUSIVELY DISTRIBUTED BY
HAL•LEONARD CORPORATION

7777 W. BLUEMOUND RD. P.O. BOX 13819 MILWAUKEE, WI 53213

Prices, contents and availability subject to change without notice.